Amazing Athletes ✧ Atletas increíbles

Shaun Alexander

Football Star ✧ Estrella del fútbol americano

Mary Ann Hoff

Traducción al español: Edua CENTRAL

PowerKiDS press & **Editorial Buenas Letras**™
New York

Published in 2007 by The Rosen Publishing Group, Inc.
29 East 21st Street, New York, NY 10010

Book Design: Daniel Hosek
Layout Design: Lissette González

Photo Credits: Cover © Harry How/Getty Images; p. 5 © Stephen Dunn/Getty Images; pp. 7, 17, 21
© Jonathan Daniel/Getty Images; p. 9 © Jamie Squire/Getty Images; p. 11 © Andy Lyons/
Getty Images; pp. 13, 19 © Otto Greule Jr./Getty Images; p. 15 © Tom Hauch/Getty Images.

Library of Congress Cataloging-in-Publication Data

Hoffman, Mary Ann, 1947-
  Shaun Alexander : football star / Mary Ann Hoffman; traducción al español: Eduardo
Alamán — 1st ed.
     p. cm. - (Amazing Athletes / Atletas increîbles)
  Includes bibliographical references and index.
  ISBN-13: 978-1-4042-7603-1
  ISBN-10: 1-4042-7603-3
  1. Alexander, Shaun. 2. Football players—United States—Biography—Juvenile literature.
  3. Running backs (Football)—United States—Biography—Juvenile literature. 4. Spanish-language
     materials I. Title. II. Series.

Manufactured in the United States of America

Shaun plays for the Seattle Seahawks. He set an NFL record of twenty-eight touchdowns in 2005.

Shaun juega en los Halcones Marinos de Seattle. En 2005, Shaun marcó 28 anotaciones. ¡Esto es un nuevo récord!

Contents

Contenido

Shaun Alexander is a running back in the NFL. NFL stands for National Football League.

Shaun Alexander juega como corredor en la NFL. La NFL, es la National Football League, que en español quiere decir Liga Nacional de Fútbol Americano.

Shaun was an important player for his college team. He holds the rushing record at his college.

Shaun fue un importante jugador en el equipo de su universidad. Shaun tiene un récord como corredor en su universidad.

In college, Shaun ran many yards and made many touchdowns. He was named Offensive Player of the Year in 1999.

En la universidad, Shaun corrió muchas yardas y logró muchas anotaciones. Shaun fue elegido Mejor Jugador Ofensivo de 1999.

Shaun was a rookie for the Seattle Seahawks in 2000. This means it was his first year in the NFL.

Shaun jugó como novato para los Halcones Marinos en 2000. Esto significa que el 2000 fue su primer año en la NFL.

13

Shaun was one of the best rushers on the Seahawks his first year. He rushed sixty-four times for 313 yards!

Shaun fue uno de los mejores corredores novatos de los Halcones Marinos. ¡En su primer año Shaun corrió sesenta y cuatro veces y logró 313 yardas!

Shaun won the MVP award for the NFL in 2005.

En 2005, Shaun fue elegido Jugador más Valioso de la NFL.

17

Shaun has played in the Pro Bowl three times. The Pro Bowl is a game played by NFL all-stars every year.

Shaun ha jugado tres veces en el Tazón de los Profesionales. En el Tazón de los Profesionales participan las estrellas de la NFL. Este partido se juega cada año.

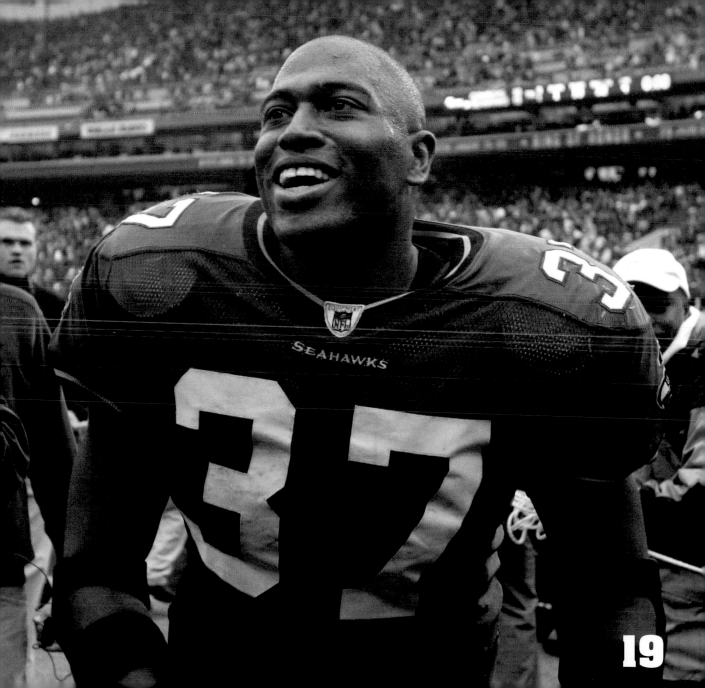

19

The Seahawks played the Pittsburgh Steelers in the 2006 Super Bowl. Shaun proved himself to be a football star!

Los Halcones Marinos jugaron contra los Acereros de Pittsburgh en el Super Tazón de 2006. ¡Shaun demostró ser una estrella del fútbol americano!

Glossary / Glosario

award (uh-WARD) A prize or honor given for something you have done.

college (KAH-lihj) A school you go to after high school.

record (REH-kurd) The best or most of something.

rush (RUSH) Running with the football.

touchdown (TUCH-down) A score made in football when a player carries or catches the ball over the other team's goal line.

---

anotación (la) Cuando un jugador lleva o atrapa la pelota dentro de la línea de meta del otro equipo.

carrera (la) Correr con el balón.

premio (el) Un reconocimiento que se le da a una persona que ha hecho algo especial.

récord (el) El mejor resultado o puntuación conseguida por una persona.

universidad (la) Una escuela a la que vas después de la escuela secundaria.

Resources / Recursos

BOOKS IN ENGLISH / LIBROS EN INGLÉS

Gibbons, Gail. *My Football Book*. Singapore: Tien Wah Press, 2000.

Mentink, Jarrett. *Alexander the Great*. Kirkland, WA: Kids in the Clouds Press, 2004.

BOOKS IN SPANISH / LIBROS EN ESPAÑOL

Suen, Anastasia. *La historia del fútbol americano*. New York: Rosen Publishing/Editorial Buenas Letras, 2004.

Index

Índice